First Published in the UK in 2016 by Focus Education (UK) Ltd
Updated September 2017

Focus Education (UK) Ltd
Publishing
Talking Point Conference & Exhibition Centre
Huddersfield Road
Scouthead
Saddleworth
OL4 4AG

Focus Education (UK) Ltd Reg. No 4507968

ISBN 978-1-909038-96-7

CW00872007

Companies, institutions and other organisations wishing to make bulk purchases of books published by Focus Education should contact their local bookstore or Focus Education direct:

Customer Services, Focus Education, Talking Point Conference & Exhibition Centre,
Huddersfield Road, Scouthead, Saddleworth, OL4 4AG
Tel 01457 821818 Fax 01457 878205

www.focus-education.co.uk
customerservice@focus-education.co.uk
Printed in Great Britain by Focus Education UK Ltd, Scouthead

focuseducationuk   focuseducation1   focus-education-uk-ltd

ABOUT THE AUTHOR

Ros Ferrara is a full-time consultant with Focus Education. This role involves leading national conferences and working with groups of schools and individual schools. She has extensive experience in all aspects of school improvement and in developing and delivering innovative training for a range of contexts and bespoke consultancy support. Ros is also an accredited Additional Inspector and undertakes Ofsted inspections on a regular basis.

Ros has 30 years experience working in a range of teaching and leadership roles in both national and international schools as well as consultant and senior leadership roles within LA advisory teams. She has also led a successful school improvement consultancy service, operating out of a federation of schools. Her work is highly valued and continues to be sought after.

Ros has written a wide range of publications. Some of Ros' most recent and best selling publications are:

- Talk in Practice: Approaches to developing talk with specific reference to EAL learners
- Grammar Writing Right
- Focus on English
- Planning for Quality Texts
- Subject Leader: English
- The place of Guided Reading in the new English Curriculum
- Grammar Games
- English Learning Challenge Curriculum: Putting Literature at the heart of the English Curriculum
- Teaching Poetry in the new National Curriculum
- Support & Challenge in Guided Reading: exemplar units from Years 1 to 6

A Guide to Moderation of Writing

End of Key Stage 1

Year 2

Working towards the expected standard	Working at the expected standard	Working at greater depth within the expected standard
The pupil can, after discussion with the teacher:	The pupil can, after discussion with the teacher:	The pupil can, after discussion with the teacher:
• write sentences that are sequenced to form a short narrative (real or fictional) • demarcate some sentences with capital letters and full stops • segment spoken words into phonemes and represent these by graphemes, spelling some words correctly and making phonically-plausible attempts at others • spell some common exception words* • form lower-case letters in the correct direction, starting and finishing in the right place • form lower-case letters of the correct size relative to one another in some of their writing • use spacing between words.	• write simple, coherent narratives about personal experiences and those of others (real or fictional) • write about real events, recording these simply and clearly • demarcate most sentences in their writing with capital letters and full stops, and use question marks correctly when required • use present and past tense mostly correctly and consistently • use co-ordination (e.g. or / and / but) and some subordination (e.g. when / if / that / because) to join clauses • segment spoken words into phonemes and represent these by graphemes, spelling many of these words correctly and making phonically-plausible attempts at others • spell many common exception words* • form capital letters and digits of the correct size, orientation and relationship to one another and to lower-case letters • use spacing between words that reflects the size of the letters.	• write effectively and coherently for different purposes, drawing on their reading to inform the vocabulary and grammar of their writing • make simple additions, revisions and proof-reading corrections to their own writing • use the punctuation taught at key stage 1 mostly correctly • spell most common exception words • add suffixes to spell most words correctly in their writing (e.g. –ment, –ness, –ful, –less, –ly) • use the diagonal and horizontal strokes needed to join some letters.

4

Year 2 Expectations

Working Towards Expected Standard	Working at the National Standard	Working at Greater Depth within the National Standard
Overall, the effectiveness and accuracy of writing is inconsistent based on the end of year expectations.	Overall, the Year 2 learning is applied effectively, accurately and independently and written texts demonstrate increasing stamina for writing.	Overall, all writing demonstrates an awareness of the reader with accurate and effective use of grammar, vocabulary. Writing is engaging and maintains the reader's interest.

Working Towards Expected Standard	Working at the National Standard	Working at Greater Depth within the National Standard
Composition and Effect		
• Writes simple narratives which have an opening, a middle and an end. • Endings are often very brief and may not relate effectively to the rest of the text. • Some of the features of non-narrative writing are used and demonstrate growing understanding of the difference between narrative and non-narrative writing. • Ideas are developed in a sequence of sentences.	• In narrative writing, there is a clear sequence of events in chronological order. • Language patterns from familiar stories may be incorporated effectively into narrative. • In non- narrative, the features of the chosen text types and appropriate sentence patterns and word choices are evident and content is sequenced effectively.	• Narrative writing is undertaken independently. • Narrative texts are clearly structured and sequenced with an opening, more developed events in sections and a better rounded ending which will relate to events in the text. • Non- narrative texts are sequenced appropriately with ideas or information developed within each section and a clear opening and closing sentence • Consistent attempts to engage the reader. • Able to sustain the writing of longer texts, showing increasing stamina.

Working Towards Expected Standard	Working at the National Standard	Working at Greater Depth within the National Standard
Structure and Organisation		
• Simple organisation reflects the purpose of the writing.	• Texts are organised according to their purpose. • Texts are structured in sections.	• The appropriate format is selected to support the organisation of the content. • Some attempts to make links between sections.

Working Towards Expected Standard	Working at the National Standard	Working at Greater Depth within the National Standard
Grammar/ Sentence Structure/ Vocabulary		

• Some sentences are extended by both subordinating and co-ordinating conjunctions.	• A variety of correctly structured sentence structures is used.	Confident and consistent use of :
	• Co-ordination and subordination are used confidently to extend ideas and add detail and information.	• Simple , compound and complex sentences
• Some different sentence types are beginning to be used for different purposes. For example, command, question etc.		• A widening variety of conjunctions to add information, expand ideas
	• The grammatical patterns of sentence types are used accurately and the sentences used purposefully.	• Different sentence types appropriate for writer's purpose and to add impact
• The appropriate tense for the purpose of the text is mostly used.		• Past and present tense, including the progressive forms
	• The appropriate tense for the purpose is used consistently, including the use of the progressive forms.	
• Expanded noun phrases, mostly by adjectives, add detail to writing.		• Word choices are thoughtful and often ambitious with specific and technical vocabulary used accurately.
	• Adverbs/adverbials are used to help sequence events and information.	
• Vocabulary choices may not always be appropriate or effective.		• Language drawn from reading is used thoughtfully and appropriately.
	• Adjectives, adverbs and expanded noun phrases are used to add detail and specify.	
		• Detail is added with the use of expanded noun phrases using adjectives, prepositional phrases and sometimes similes.
	• Word choices are thoughtful and sometimes ambitious with specific or technical vocabulary used in non-narrative writing.	
		• Adverbials are used to sequence writing and occasionally to show a change in setting.

Working Towards Expected Standard	Working at the National Standard	Working at Greater Depth within the National Standard
Punctuation		
• Sentences are usually demarcated by capital letters and full stops. • Capital letters for names and personal pronoun I are used consistently and independently. • Beginning to use question marks and exclamation marks, realising their effect on the reader. • Some use of commas to separate items in a list. • Some attempt at use of apostrophe for contraction and singular possession.	• Capital letters and full stops are mostly used to demarcate sentences. • Question marks are used accurately. • Capital letters are used for the personal pronoun I and for most proper nouns. • Commas are used to separate items in a list. • Apostrophes are used to mark contractions. • Apostrophes for singular possession are sometimes used correctly.	Confident and consistent use of: • Capital letters and appropriate end marks to demarcate sentences. • Capital letters for the personal pronoun I and for proper nouns. • Commas are used to separate items in a list. • Apostrophes to mark contractions. • Apostrophes for singular possession.

Working Towards Expected Standard	Working at the National Standard	Working at Greater Depth within the National Standard
Drafting/ Editing and Proof Reading		
• Writing is re-read for editing and proof reading when prompted. • Changes to improve writing are made with prompting and adult support.	• Writing is re-read to check for meaning. • Changes are made to improve the effect and impact sometimes independently and sometimes in discussion with an adult. • Writing is proof read for accuracy with some guidance.	• Writing is re-read and its effectiveness evaluated independently. • Changes are made to improve the impact. • Proof reading is careful and inaccuracies corrected mostly independently.

Working Towards Expected Standard	Working at the National Standard	Working at Greater Depth within the National Standard
Spelling and Handwriting		
• Most common exception words spelled accurately. • Some evidence that the spelling rules and patterns from Year 2 are beginning to be used correctly. • Lower case and capital letters are formed and oriented mostly correctly.	• Most common exception words spelled accurately. • Spelling rules and patterns from Year 2 are being used with increasing accuracy. • Capital letters and lower case letters are correctly sized and oriented • Diagonal and horizontal strokes needed to join letters are used in some writing • Upper and lower case letters are not mixed within words.	• Common exception words spelled accurately. • Spelling rules and patterns from Year 2 are applied accurately with spelling strategies used to attempt more ambitious words. • Capital letters and lower case letters are correctly sized and oriented and most letters are joined.

A Guide to Moderation of Writing

End of Key Stage 2

Year 6

Working towards the expected standard	Working at the expected standard	Working at greater depth within the expected standard
The pupil can: • write for a range of purposes • use paragraphs to organise ideas • in narratives, describe settings and characters • in non-narrative writing, use simple devices to structure the writing and support the reader (e.g. headings, sub-headings, bullet points) • use capital letters, full stops, question marks, commas for lists and apostrophes for contraction mostly correctly • spell correctly most words from the year 3 / year 4 spelling list, and some words from the year 5 / year 6 spelling list* • write legibly.1	The pupil can: • write effectively for a range of purposes and audiences, selecting language that shows good awareness of the reader (e.g. the use of the first person in a diary; direct address in instructions and persuasive writing) • in narratives, describe settings, characters and atmosphere • integrate dialogue in narratives to convey character and advance the action • select vocabulary and grammatical structures that reflect what the writing requires, doing this mostly appropriately (e.g. using contracted forms in dialogues in narrative; using passive verbs to affect how information is presented; using modal verbs to suggest degrees of possibility) • use a range of devices to build cohesion (e.g. conjunctions, adverbials of time and place, pronouns, synonyms) within and across paragraphs • use verb tenses consistently and correctly throughout their writing • use the range of punctuation taught at key stage 2 mostly correctly (e.g. inverted commas and other punctuation to indicate direct speech) • spell correctly most words from the year 5 / year 6 spelling list,* and use a dictionary to check the spelling of uncommon or more ambitious vocabulary • maintain legibility in joined handwriting when writing at speed	The pupil can: • write effectively for a range of purposes and audiences, selecting the appropriate form and drawing independently on what they have read as models for their own writing (e.g. literary language, characterisation, structure) • distinguish between the language of speech and writing and choose the appropriate register • exercise an assured and conscious control over levels of formality, particularly through manipulating grammar and vocabulary to achieve this • use the range of punctuation taught at key stage 2 correctly (e.g. semi-colons, dashes, colons, hyphens) and, when necessary, use such punctuation precisely to enhance meaning and avoid ambiguity [There are no additional statements for spelling or handwriting]

Year 6 Expectations

Working Towards Expected Standard	Working at the National Standard	Working at Greater Depth within the National Standard
Overall pupils' writing may lack consistency. It may demonstrate some of the features of the expected standard, but there will be insufficient control, some basic errors in accuracy and inconsistencies in application.	Overall, pupils' writing will be accurate and effective. Features of the expected standard will be controlled and used purposefully and accurately. Written texts will be well-crafted and engaging.	Overall, writing is independent and all elements of the Year 6 curriculum are consistently and effectively applied appropriately to produce engaging, sustained and well-crafted texts.

Working Towards Expected Standard	Working at the National Standard	Working at Greater Depth within the National Standard
	# Composition and Effect	

<table>
<tr>
<td valign="top">

- Can write a range of texts for different purposes and different audiences.

- The features of the chosen text type are used appropriately for the purpose and the identified audience.

- In narrative writing:

- Effective settings, characters, atmosphere and plots are created.
- Dialogue is used to show character and to move events forward although there may be some over-use.

- In non –narrative writing:

- An appropriate style and vocabulary is used to maintain the reader's interest.

- Appropriate choices are sometimes made between informal and formal language dependent on the purpose and audience of the text.

- The text has a recognisable viewpoint or voice which may not always be sustained throughout.

- Conclusions may attempt to relate subject to reader or make direct appeal to reader. However, endings may be the weakest element of the whole text.

</td>
<td valign="top">

- Can write a range of effective texts for different purposes and different audiences.

- Text types are well-chosen and used appropriately for the purpose and the identified audience.

In narrative writing:

- Descriptions of settings, characters and atmosphere are used appropriately
- Dialogue is used successfully to convey character and move events forward in combination with action and description
- Narrative techniques such as flashbacks and shifts in time are used to maintain the reader's interest

In non –narrative writing:

- An appropriate style and vocabulary is used dependent on the text type and is used successfully to entertain, inform or persuade.

- Appropriate choices are mostly made between informal and formal language dependent on the purpose and audience of the text.

- Viewpoint is well controlled and convincing. Texts have a clear voice which is sustained.

- Openings are varied and appropriate for the purpose of the text. They engage, and at times, may directly address the reader.

- Closings are well thought out and conclude texts effectively. They may, for example, make direct comment on the content, pose a question, make a direct link to the opening or reflect a change in a character.

</td>
<td valign="top">

- Writing has clear voice which is evident across all texts.

- A range of writing for different purposes and audiences. The features and conventions of a text type may be used unconventionally or manipulated to create specific effects.

- The influence of reading is evident in thoughtful use of literary techniques and devices.

- Levels of formality are established, used appropriately and sustained and add to the effectiveness and impact of the writing.

</td>
</tr>
</table>

Working Towards Expected Standard	Working at the National Standard	Working at Greater Depth within the National Standard
	Structure and Organisation	
• Paragraphs are used to organise ideas. • Ideas are developed and elaborated on within paragraphs. • Fronted adverbials are used to link ideas between paragraphs and sometimes within paragraphs. • Pronouns are also sometimes used to support cohesion in and between paragraphs. • Dialogue, action and description are used appropriately. However, this may be unbalanced with over emphasis of one element. • Appropriate organisational and presentational devices are used to structure text dependent on the purpose and audience.	• The selected structure is carefully controlled throughout the text which maintains and emphasises its context and purpose. • Paragraphs with clear topic sentences are used to guide the reader so that texts are well-shaped and follow a clear and coherent sequence. • Paragraphs are developed and expand ideas, information, opinions, descriptions, themes and events in depth with relevant detail. • A range of cohesive devices is used to link ideas within and across paragraphs. For example, repetition of words, phrases or sentences, adverbials, including conjunctive adverbs, generalisers and verb tenses or forms. • Elements of dialogue, action and description are interwoven appropriately to support text structure, move events forward and maintain the reader's interest • Appropriate organisational and presentational devices are used to structure text dependent on the purpose and audience.	• Paragraphing is precise and used to structure texts. • Paragraphs are used to develop and expand ideas or points of view, themes and events in depth. • A varied range of cohesive devices is used across and within paragraphs. • They may vary in length according to the writer's purpose.

Working Towards Expected Standard	Working at the National Standard	Working at Greater Depth within the National Standard

Grammar/ Sentence Structure/ Vocabulary

• A variety of simple, compound and complex sentences is used and mostly controlled to create impact and effect.	• Variety of simple, compound and complex sentences is used with control to indicate levels of informality and formality and to create particular effects.	• Dependent on the audience, purpose and context, writing demonstrates confident, controlled and effective use of:
• The use of complex sentences is mostly secure with some variation of the position of the clause, included embedding clauses.	• Positioning and manipulation of clauses in complex and multi-clause sentences is varied to shift emphasis or focus for effect and impact.	• Sentences containing more than one clause are used to elaborate and to convey complicated information concisely
• Attempts to construct more ambitious, multi-clause sentences may not always be controlled and result in lack of clarity	• Relative clauses, which draw on a range of relative pronouns and adverbs, are used to clarify information and to add detail.	• Precise vocabulary and grammatical choices including the deliberate use of the passive voice to affect the presentation of information in both formal and informal situations and the subjunctive mood as appropriate
• Range of verbs forms is used mostly accurately. This may include attempts, which are only successful sometimes, to use modality to position an argument and the passive voice to shift focus.	• Tense is chosen to support the cohesion of the text.	• Varied, precise, appropriate and often ambitious vocabulary is used
• Grammatical structures used do not always reflect the level of formality required for the purpose and audience of the text.	• Range of verbs forms are used accurately and to create more subtle meanings.	• A range of literary features add to the impact of the text. For example, repetition, short sentences, figurative language.
• Noun phrases are expanded by adjectives, prepositional phrases and adverbials to add detail to sentences. This detail may sometimes lack purpose and precision	• Modal verbs and adverbs are used to position an argument as well as to indicate degrees of possibility, probability and certainty.	• Levels of formality are controlled through selecting vocabulary precisely and by manipulating grammatical structures
	• Passive voice is used to affect the focus or presentation of information in a sentence.	

Working Towards Expected Standard	Working at the National Standard	Working at Greater Depth within the National Standard

Grammar/ Sentence Structure/ Vocabulary (continued)

• Adverbials, including conjunctive adverbs are used as cohesive devices. These may be basic, repeated or used inappropriately at times. • Vocabulary choices are often imaginative. • Technical vocabulary is usually used appropriately. • Some vocabulary choices may not reflect the level of formality required for the purpose and audience of the writing.	• Subjunctive mood may be used in very formal contexts. • Expanded noun phrases are used to be specific and add effective detail and description.as well as to convey complicated information with precision. • Adverbials, including conjunctive adverbs are used as cohesive devices. These are used precisely to open paragraphs, to change point of view as well as to add detail. • Vocabulary choices are imaginative and words are used precisely and appropriately to create impact and enhance meaning. This includes choice of verbs to show and not tell and to describe as well as qualifying adverbs. • Technical vocabulary is selected appropriately. • Word choices are made to reflect the level of formality.	

Working Towards Expected Standard	Working at the National Standard	Working at Greater Depth within the National Standard

Punctuation

• Used mostly accurately: • capital letters • full stops • question marks • exclamation marks • commas for lists • commas for fronted adverbials • apostrophes for contractions • inverted commas • Attempts to use other forms of punctuation which may not be accurate: • dash • comma to demarcate clauses, including in dialogue • colon • semi-colon • Use of commas insecure and may be used incorrectly in place of full stops.	• Used mostly accurately: • inverted commas • commas for lists • commas for fronted adverbials • commas for clauses, including the reporting clause in dialogue • punctuation for parenthesis • semi-colon to introduce a list • brackets for parenthesis • • Sometimes used accurately: • semi-colons to mark boundaries between independent clauses • colons to mark boundaries between independent clauses • dashes to mark boundaries between independent clauses • hyphens • Use of the comma is secure with only infrequent errors and comma splices.	• The complete range of punctuation is used mostly correctly, including: • semi-colons to mark the boundary between independent clauses • colons to mark the boundary between independent clauses • The use of the comma is secure. • Punctuation clarifies the intended meaning

Working Towards Expected Standard	Working at the National Standard	Working at Greater Depth within the National Standard
Drafting/ Editing and Proof Reading		
• Evidence of changes made independently when re-drafting or editing. Changes may sometimes lack careful thought and may not add to the effectiveness of the writing. • Second drafts may look very similar to first drafts. • Evidence of application of feedback from peers or adults. • Independent proof reading may lack precision. • Proof reading is effective and accuracy is checked only when guided or directed to particular areas.	• Second drafts show evaluative and reflective thinking which is evidenced by thoughtful and effective changes made to create effects and to impact on the reader. • Many changes will be effected independently. • There will also be clear evidence over time of application and use of feedback from peers and adults. • Proof reading is mostly effective and the usage of spelling, punctuation and grammar is checked for accuracy and consistency.	• The drafting process is used efficiently and second drafts or edited work show carefully considered changes or amendments to enhance meaning, create impact or aid precision. • Writing is evaluated as a matter of course. • Proof reading ensures a high level of accuracy.

Working Towards Expected Standard	Working at the National Standard	Working at Greater Depth within the National Standard

Spelling and Handwriting

• Most words spelled correctly from Year 3 and 4 list.	• Most words spelled correctly from Year 5 and 6 list.	• Spelling is mainly accurate with only occasional errors in more ambitious vocabulary.
• Some words spelled correctly from Year 5 and 6 list.	• Spelling strategies and the range of spelling rules and patterns from KS2 are applied accurately.	• Legible, fluent handwriting is mostly maintained with a personal style evident.
• Common exception words spelled correctly.	• Handwriting is fluent and legible with a personal style in which decisions may have been made whether or not to join specific letters.	
• Spelling rules and patterns from Years 1, 2, 3 and 4 mostly applied correctly.		
• Spelling rules and patterns from Years 5 and 6 sometimes applied correctly.		
• Handwriting is legible and mostly joined.		